ANABRANCH

WESLEYAN POETRY

ANABRANCH

Andrew Zawacki

Wesleyan University Press

MIDDLETOWN, CONNECTICUT

Published by Wesleyan University Press,

Middletown, CT 06459

© 2004 by Andrew Zawacki

Printed in the Unites States of America

5 4 3 2 1

LIBRARY OF CONGRESS CATALOGING-IN-PUBLICATION DATA

Zawacki, Andrew, 1972–

Anabranch / Andrew Zawacki.

   p.   cm. — (Wesleyan poetry)

Includes bibliographical references.

ISBN 0–8195–6700–0 (cloth : alk. paper) — ISBN 0–8195–6701–9
(pbk. : alk. paper)

I. Title. II. Series.

PS3626.A93A85 2004

813'.6—dc22   2004000496

To my mother & father

CONTENTS

Grateful acknowledgments are due to the editors of the following, where versions of these poems first appeared: *American Letters & Commentary, Arena Magazine, Boston Review, Bridge, Common Knowledge, Denver Quarterly, Euphony, Fence, Gulf Coast, The Iowa Review, Jacket, The Kenyon Review, Konture, Meanjin, Metre, New American Writing, The New Yorker, No: a journal of the arts, The Red Wheelbarrow, River City, Slope, Third Coast, TriQuarterly, Untitled, Upstairs at Duroc,* and *Volt.*

Masquerade was originally published as a Stray Dog Editions chapbook by the Vagabond Press in Sydney (2001), under the editorship of Michael Brennan. Selections appeared subsequently in *Józef Wittlin & Modern Polish and Polish-American Poetry: A Commemorative Anthology,* edited by Piotr Gwiazda for the Polish Cultural Institute in New York City (2001), and in *Great American Prose Poems: From Poe to the Present,* edited by David Lehman and published by Scribner (2003). My gratitude to C. D. Wright and the Poetry Society of America, for awarding the sequence the 2002 Alice Fay Di Castagnola Award. The first section of "Viatica" received the 2002 Cecil Hemley Memorial Award, thanks to Wayne Koestenbaum and the PSA. "Credo" was printed as a broadside to commemorate Dialogue Through Poetry Week and UNESCO's World Poetry Day in Paris (2003), *grâce à* Ethan Gilsdorf.

I am indebted to these organizations, for their generosity: the Committee on Social Thought at the University of Chicago, the J. William Fulbright Foreign Scholarship Board, the Australian-American Fulbright Commission, the Lois Roth Endowment, the Centre for Comparative Literature and Cultural Studies at Monash University, and the Australian Centre at the University of Melbourne. Thank you to Robert Pippin, Evelyn Nef, and the Evelyn Nef Steffanson Foundation, for your support.

My personal thanks go to Carrie Adams, Bob Adamson, Judith Bishop, Karin Christiansen, Aleš Debeljak, Mike Farrell, Forrest Gander, Sandrine Garet, Kevin and Rita Hart, Luke Haynes, Kristin Headlam, Mike Heller, Bryce Johnson, John Koethe, Scott Lindsey, Rhyll and Al Nance, Adam Novy, Jon Novy, Bin Ramke, Josh Ruxin, Gustaf Sobin, Mark Strand, Suzanna Tamminen, Chris Wallace-Crabbe, and Benjamin Zawacki. And especially Brian Henry: *When the mind is like a hall in which thought is like a voice speaking, the voice is always that of some one else.*

ANABRANCH

Credo

You say wind is only wind
& carries nothing nervous
in its teeth.
      I do not believe it.

I have seen leaves desist
         from moving
although the branches
      move, & I
believe a cyclone has secrets
the weather is ignorant of.
        I believe
in the violence of not knowing.

I've seen a river lose its course
& join itself again,
      watched it court
a stream & coax the stream
into its current,

      & I have seen
rivers, not unlike
      you, that failed to find
their way back.
      I believe the rapport
between water & sand, the advent
from mirror to face.

      I believe in rain
to cover what mourns,

in hail that revives
& sleet that erodes, believe
whatever falls
is a figure of rain

& now I believe in torrents that take
everything down with them.

The sky calls it quits,
or so I believe,
when air, or earth, or air
has had enough.

I believe in disquiet,
the pressure it plies, believe a cloud
to govern the limits of night.

I say I,
but little is left to say it, much less
mean it—
& yet I do.

Let there be
no mistake:
I do not believe
things are reborn in fire.
They're consumed by fire

& the fire has a life of its own.

Viatica

.

alone and in advance
over an unknown grave:

the moon, the moonlight, side of the moon
that leans against a dark the dark leans on:

would last and it would last, and the sound
it makes would not be lasting sound

but only noise a sun gives off
en route to something other than itself:

and the night would last, one side
of night, dissolving a language

that leans on the dark, on trees and men
who walk like trees, before before

as winter would last: winterstricken
a wayward moon, and gravity at long

at last, and how it would aggravate, how
dissolve, and how a tree resembling a detour

would understay its welcome: noise before
the dark before, and men who walk

with eyes ajar, one side of their eyes
advancing alone, trees as doctrinaire

as dark, and men whose language
only the moon stands under:

who take this splintered otherwise
for a life that will not last

snow today and through tomorrow
and through tomorrow night, in a stutter

the logic of dominos, music the method
of dice: northsouth and isterdriven

do not tarry, do not turn, because
the impartial, because because:

gigolo heat and the haze it chafes against
encrypted blue, a prayer for their sickness

that went, that went: the salt of x
is the psalm of x, encoded in apricot,

gunpowder tea, and given
to being given again and against:

I owe myself, I owe myself,
dancing in front of the doorway my debt,

dancing in front of it, open or shut

3

for instance this broken
mirror I call my savior (my sinister)

where did she come from (where will she)
when wrong the way to follow

nothing but less than less (and listen low):
for who will pour the red approximate

red we meant when we sang never
never riddance all the same (nothing

is the same): tunebroke lapidaria,
where art thou, my love (lascivia

mine), where this day in spring
(in summertime): o hiding

behind rain from the south
as beauty doth modest hide, in nearings

of a leaden, awkward north (we stay
averse): so north ourselves inside a lurid

sunbeam's dusty glow, across the fields
we'll go (we'll go), over rocks and grass,

just ten cents between us (but the whole
wide world ahead) and this tiny glass

jig we whistle o no (o no)
(jig we whistle o no)

4   (Albedo)

: withheld in evidence

: the inessential first

: no other other
  no other enamor

: ad hoc this love to the end of the line
  a taciturn stratagem

: costumed inadvertent

: cited at the name

: name of the other
  name of the of

: weighted and found wanting

: this unaccustomed light

5

this the partition and this
its departure: a language that limped

with death inside, an angel, a fire,
an angel, a foe: and a name

that limped with a name inside
and rested between us, wresting

us from us: edgewater and a cappella,
pillar of cloudwarp, pillar of fear,

and whithersoever a scapegrace
flees the voice that fled from him:

no one of cerement, no one of caul,
recursive in a tailored wind

that shuttles back and forth
across the bay: the sun was the sun

and the moon was the sun, and he
was a cloud of witness unto the sun,

the scald, a chorus of sunlight,
the faithlessness of its veer:

o sorrow of cobalt o sainfoin
o stone, this current that picks up trash

as it crawls, to scatter it farther down
along the coast: with death inside,

both of us deathward,
angel my enemy, nowhere my name

6

who followed himself and forgot
himself, and when the way forward

was minted in soot, as midnight
unlocked its arms, who counterfeited

the garroted path, then counter-
feited himself: who washed himself

and washed himself, with snow water,
water of diamond, water from the ice

that water had made: who could not
come clean, with mudsalve, with rain,

saliva on the eyes and on the throat:
who kerned himself and his messages

to one without number or name,
arrowed himself, unfigured himself,

pulled apart the voice he couldn't see
and turned to see, and could not see:

who promised himself to rabid dust,
rising with storm feints, rising without,

promised himself to the faience
under his feet: was told he would

find it, not need to look, told
he'd recognize what came upon him

in the open, its shattered limbs
and urgent, osseous light: who

called it *encaustic*, called it *alas*,
said it was somewhere the wind

couldn't bend: and who, having never
been there, would go there again

7   (Albedo)

: or else or else
  the elsewhere is not   any place other than here

: to wait for a call
  a call will not come   and in its not coming is here

: she is a difference
  the sky is the sky   between marks a difference here

: never in tinted glass
  in tarnish   corridor each end of which

: the lover not over   the lover not here

: these are fragile
  and these are fragile   surrenders what it does not have

: fleabane and boneset   remainder remainder

: fleabane and boneset   where if not here

8

still it lacked the imperious
antecedent, a misspelled word

that signaled another word
to render us by: half jade, half jet,

octobering into the afterleave
on improvise and ache, the sound

we make when scraped against
each other: you who guard

the errant of your letter, I
who can't get rid of what I've got

9

anapest flowers, courtyard of ash,
shadow that casts a slattern, peridot sun

and fronts that come in and keep going:
a seethrough woman, a man with a face

and a man with a frost harmonica,
settling his score with the sun:

razorgrass, razorgrass,
remember my shape and my shiver:

when next I lay me down to sleep
I'll be under you—

a sapphire woman, a man cut
from glass, and women who dance

on the verge of themselves, garnet
and gossamer wives who pass

through flame: saying *sunshine,*
sunshine, and blowing painted kisses

to the painted, several suns

one of me stuttered and one
of me broke, and one of me tried

to fasten a line to one of
me untying it from me:

one of me watched a fisherman haul
a sand shark from the breaker,

while another was already years later,
returned to where a local man

baited for striper but landed a shark:
one of me sat under olivine clouds,

clouds of cerise, a courtesan sky,
and one of me sunned himself

as a child, imagining a fish rod
turned fermata: one waved a sash

of cornflower blue, one heard
a windmill, one heard the wind,

one waved goodbye to an imminent,
leftover love: and one strolled

barefoot and sunburnt across
the nickel inhibitions of afternoon,

tossing amber bottles at a smoke tree,
the gun lake, swimming toward

his family on the dock as twilight fell,
as the same boy stayed behind

to look at him swim: one believed
a father could be killed by falling rock,

and one woke up to find he'd only
dreamt, although his father was dead,

and one believed in a beautiful house
not built by any hand: one promised

nothing would break, and nothing did,
and one saw breaking everywhere

and could not say what he saw

take these hands and the sever
they harbor, for they will not break

or deliver us from, and take this falter
that shelters a stress, for death is neither

broken nor taken back: take, too,
the intimate stranger, who cannot

be broken by ardors he bears,
who takes whatever is riven asunder

and glues it back together, solder
or lock: and take this specter

of vis-à-vis, the errors he ventures,
the window, the sill, and take his sister,

parergon to never, who crosses over
the uglier bridge in order to look

at the beautiful, broken one: likewise
the figure in lamplight and rain,

take his umbrella, the profile it strikes,
take what courts a final encounter

behind the repair garage: brassknuckle,
pistolwhip, take his arms before they tire,

pity on what he pays for
with his face: striptease and uppercut,

after a shot glass, after a room, slivers
of icon and afterward, take the neighbor

who buries what he finds: a red
flower, a good thrashing, a white

and wooden overcoat, the end of,
the exit of, that nobody wore,

no one even wore

one by one the architraves, they were part
of the falling snow, and one by one

these brothers of mine, who walk
on broken feet through falling snow:

and the women my mouth evented to
who slept inside the snow, one by one

their lips on salted glass, its opulent glare,
and the hair they left to be forgotten by:

and one by one the pallid restorations
of my sight, its orange trees and wisteria

took part in the staging of snow, even if
nothing resembled the lithium snow:

one by one the visitors saying
fuck you, I don't remember,

I can't feel my face,
vanishing into a fever, a falling,

my namesake every one, and under
the book of ignition another book

to offer us up, who stand beneath
ourselves to seek ourselves:

vertigo, vertigo,
wherever you go I also will go

and we will be part of the falling
if not a part of the snow—

and stillborn a verdelho sky, one by one
its bezeled hypotheses, all of them wrong,

and one by one the nascent, the near
occasion of, opening my open eyes, and only

snow had nothing to do with the snow

13

debonair this ivorycut, days
I'm one and more than one,

cavalier and less than one,
as what I thought was water

starts to burn: nights that leave me
unlived in, apart, and night

that pins all giving, all ground,
citrine light and scaffold to its lapel:

amnesia, amnesia, haunted by
this breath of another, from outside,

outside, by dint of interruption,
awake with no reprieve: serrated

by hairweed, cartilage, bone,
the beach dissolves to agar and ink,

night divesting the ocean of its curt
and violet pledge, its plainsong

married to winter, pumiced and un-
beknownst: impasse my passage,

terminus, terminus, breathe upon
the living, the blind, the not yet

and no longer, upon this O
of difference pointing *there*—

     do you see it, friend?

Albedo

And now as broken glasses show
A hundred lesser faces
                    —John Donne

1

To hold your breath & keep breathing

The bended light
a fractured pulse

Lake with interior sun

Auditing the afternoon
its integers of blue

robin's egg   riffraff
scissor   vagabond

Who are you
& why are you drowning

Quiet to witness
quiet to rise

Put your hand through lexicons
of solitude & surrender

2

Breath that builds a cinquefoil cloud
by flooding another breath

Why I cannot remember

Intentioned   anonymous

Ask me if I am a prism

Ask where I hung
what little I own

Cannot tell sun
from shadows it steals

Ask me why I lost the way
I was

3   (Vertigo)

If wind that wastes its time among the trees
escapes itself, only to end up quarantined
by a derelict squall from the north,

and if the air turns somersaults, miming
the outtakes of dusk, scandaled by an early frost
and punished for its coldness by the cold—

then, like a bullet that lodges in bone,
becoming a piece of the body,
you will not awake apart from your name.

And I will not be not a part of you.

4

Another one   the one called I

goes back & forth
pretending not to hear

Ricochet & replica

A moth-eaten garment

A dress on the floor

Never warp too far
(Caesura)

No   the river is ice

Do not leave

Chauffeur my ruins

Do not leave me

Custodial white

A syncope at the heart
that rubrics in half

Not   mirage   do not

5   (Vertigo)

There are things I would settle
with myself. Why, for instance,
as autumn unravels, I cannot mortar

myself to myself, nothing but sunlight
littered from here to the sun. By I
I mean a window, redness grazing the lake

at dawn, or an echo winnowing out
along a wall, hard pressed to hide itself
and straining for the voice it vanished from.

I mean so many windows. So much red.

6

So what
the colors are fading

(Pause)   (resume)
from tearing astray

Updown   updown

O speak of not enough
nothing

Say the wind
will hurry your mouth

toward me
& once was me

Say what shape a damaged ruse

Tell me this rip
is a wave going out

Be anagram my only

For now
at least for now

7

Until the dark begins to lift

Hastened from door to door

Doctor   she said
it's so nice to see you

This is how I loved   awoke
eyes   (as in) I closed my

Tattoo   (pause on the stair)

Rowing a boat in another's room
faltering under the trees

What part of night was theirs
& why

Island after island

If only edges

To share for a while

Unmoored corner   my archer
my open

Pause if you will on the stair

Until the dark   to lift

8

& like a sea that mounts resilience
minutes before a storm

her eyes   & the green of her eyes

& the storms they put to grind
inside me

9

Leave undone the cypresses

Leave undone the salt

Leave the orange of after
& sepia flaring dusk

Leave alone the cinders

the pond & its conspiracy
of cigarette packs & plastic

Leave the gasoline as it rumors the barn

Leave the hemophiliac sun
that wears itself out

keeps wearing out

Leave the row of plane trees
to its perfume of decay

(Someone shields a match against the rain
as if to say

go)

10   (Vertigo)

Please do not misunderstand.
That woman who carries winter
inside her, dizzied by snowfall

that won't level off—I would say
I love her, but I is too strong a word
and love not strong enough.

11

Whatever the winter
razors a window

Ever the clock with its nihil
& nerve

Field of   (the hotel aflame)

River that carries everything off

Water as rupture   water at rest

River leaving everything intact

Fold of   (no)   (no)

Hold me together I'm
cracking

The sea has not fallen

The sea has not fallen

(Offstage whisper)

The sea has not fallen

One believed in a beautiful house

Nowhere & never & falling

I brought a heart into the room but from

(Take these hands)   (put your hand)

The room I carried none with me

The beautiful   the broken one

Not built by any hand

Until the dark   to lift the dark

As light will fever glass that fevers light

Masquerade

One differing in itself
—Heraclitus

Whether sunlight opened the spaces it fell on, allowing the gum trees their differences, twisted aquas and shaved, quixotic papyrus, or whether the clearing was already there, touching dawn and the limits it altered, granting the sun a figure by which it was tagged, or conceived by the eyes of those it still mattered to, the afternoon about to happen could not elaborate: its adroit but seemingly random distinctions—the river as something other than its banks, water discrete from roiling and silt—were presences with a difficult origin, part of the apparatus of waking and not outside the day or how it developed. The articulation of shadow to fence, of bridge to the parklands it parsed and interviewed, enlisted itself inside questions without any curve. Yet to follow them was our valence, and in that abandon sheltered a reason for why, though unbeknownst to each other, and unknown even to those we kept calling our selves.

2

November unfolded its bones on the moors, a scatter of lacus-
trine snow. Hiking a breakaway ridge, we marked the feats of
a deafening promise, the terms of which had long since been
revoked: afternoon-midnight, summer-winter, yesterday-to-
morrow, a single pressure standing in for all permutations
and routes. The wind picked up and put us ahead of evasion,
and the signals we listened for but didn't hear, trickling along
the no-trespassing placards, branches tipped with sheens of
loosened sky, were pilfered from sled runs covering over, from
whiteout and lackluster frost, from downpour and dust, from
way before.

3

Yet what did light have to do with the outskirts it lay along?
It urged more than mere decoration, obsidian arouse, as night
drew near the water pump and died off. In the fern gully, at
the end of a driveway inclined with brambles unhauled af-
ter yesterday's hacking, blackwood and wattle attended what
stars slithered down, exchanging each other for vistas the
rooms set adrift: nothing belonged to the tin cans and rooks,
slipshod signposts that vines had overgrown and refused to
release, flowerpots that got moved while we turned in our
bunks, dreaming of thieves. Decreation was legislated, an or-
dinance of brush-burning and regrowth after the ashes blew
afield. A house enameled in stained glass and stone, soaked
with a late hour's hosing of all the wood and window frames,
a fire that surrounded, leapt over the roof, curtsy of a lake-
front at the meadow's farthest end—not without fervor and
not without us.

4

Return was a myth departure coined as incentive—we didn't believe it, bracken and twig, but moved ahead anyway. Negotiating winter's frisk and what remained of its pane, worn away by powerlines and barns the rain brought down, we kept to where the sun revamped its reach: upholstered clouds and amassings of geese, making their exodus vocal, mountains that seemed to change their position, ruptures in the road the crews ignored, before defaulting to some other damage control. It would not have been false to conjure transparence or zero, to coax the sight of scaffolds ghosting white pine, ilex, tea tree, birch. The metabolism of snowshoe and compass: nothing could stall it or usher it onward, not when it had already been stated, and called us so we came.

5

Lightning and suddenly everything rendered, stricken into relief: rosellas zagging from guardrail to limb, from telephone wire to the trailers it linked, bellbirds scudding an atmosphere of stormclouds roaming in, unbidden but adamant showers close behind. These were the margins we swore we'd not tamper with, as dampness engaged its intention, or allow to be displaced by a scission dividing us too: a car without wheels at the side of the yard, rusting into the night until nighttime itself, cordon of timber for months without warmth or caesura. Standing between two modes of indifference and flight, we held the kitchen door ajar, in case of whatever else might need to depart, if not to preserve a silence fogging windows in the wake of the already gone; while the patio door, at back of this home no longer a home, shuddered in gusts that neither ascribed nor hid, but offered a scent. Had there been someone who slept through the onslaught, collar turned up at the exit of even himself, we'd have heard him calling out for the women he never loved, traipsing from sun to sun in a stowaway wind.

6

The docks had been taken apart for the season, plank by plank, washer by bolt, and kids would earn extra cash, come spring, for putting them back out. The casino three miles over was boarded up, fast food and faster girls a cure for midsummer malaise, since winter meant bus stops and work, if any, and lunch in one of the lodges near the church. We walked where the boats had been, no trace of the floating names this brittle water was otherwise painted: To Carry On Conversation With Houses, Whomsoever They Do Not Recognize, What We Saw We Leave Behind While What We Did Not See Or Catch We Take With Us Away. In flannel and fluorescent hunting vests, men drilled holes in matte chautauqua ice, thermoses raised against wind that gnawed their cigarettes like a bone, plumbing with hooklines for anything underneath. Skaters leaned as if weightlessness could erase intaglio, then lifted above the scrolls their blades had whittled and fuzzed into glare: to untie the letters from lamps they'd hung off, longer than anyone knew.

Casuarinas kept time, or did not keep it but gave it away, betraying how midday waned into moonswipe, bestowing upon the visible these guessed-at charges from somewhere less so. Echolalia, except no one had spoken, yet nevertheless the leaves were being swayed if not persuaded. The old hotel on the strand, the green of its shutters flaked from not being opened or closed by anyone living, insured a separation between hills that harbored a secret of staying and tides that tended to balk, bickering with sand and busted shells, with trash that catamarans coughed up or tailgaters ditched despite fines. The arabesques and curlicues of afterhours and charcoal: we heard glasses clinking on the deck in slurred uncertainty, waiters threading tables, sprinting downstairs for a smoke or a kiss, a call on the line about where to be later, after the barstools were turned. For now the dumpster lids would stay open, the hose uncoiled, tarp tied back. Restraint was a key in a lock and an unfinished bottle, palm trees like frozen fireworks.

8

Spirit-lamp, spirit-level, tain by which the face would aspire to horizon. Gulls rehearsing plié and plummet, little stuffed in the bins to irk their attention, the barge split purplewater and crest, zipping up immodestly behind. Say there had been a bridge to the island, somewhere to stand when the wharf-lights eased on, to drop our styrofoam cups and watch them falter in the furl: we might have witnessed the fishmongers bustling, battening their stalls, or sirens moaning C-minor ahead of the gale. As it happened, we read the hurricane into whatever history would vouch, or perhaps we wrote it down, for others to believe. Neap tide lanced and haltered, morph-ing into requiems of quarto, octavo, inkwell and quill, the violins resuscitating what mimes had trouble staging in the square: that we had not existed, nor would we ever again.

9

A woman who stirred from the fret of a wave, its gaunt, aristocratic collapse. And red rising out of red: a mountain with a larynx, a lung.

Leaving no sooner it already motioned divergence, occurring from another place, a separate verb, over here: a singular axis emanating order, furze bush abstaining a lurch into flame, foxglove and the coquettish breeze it answered to by noon. To quicken, dally, almost envision: fusebox inundated with images, the factory burnished a sterile, tentative gloss, chainlink and crumbling brick draped in hand-me-down revolver blue, passage into those we could neither forsake nor apportion a pledge. Incursions, we called them, qualified: wayward cancellations of an asphalt parking garage, a death's-head moth hellbent on halogen spokes. Loading bays a narthex to cavalier guesswork, we stumbled past pretending not to notice, not to need, though even Orion's makeshift belt, not where it was when we'd jinxed its elisions, splayed three halves of heaven, and no two alike.

The drowned from their drawing rooms: lost inside a still-life by someone who never saw them, not even the daughter who stayed for a while, leaving again before sun-up. Dissolving on iron staircases, pulled by the gravel to reckon: a lieutenant from the wedge brigade, or the widow he exiled not least from herself, seven sisters wrapped in a voile of coral labyrinths and salt. Skipping stones on cobbled backstreets, saying nothing to no one, we squinted through gasps of longitude and dates the decades had rubbed, knowing like a swimmer who waits for the beach to keep inching close: soon it would be time to go home, and pretend that all of this would be penciled in, or forgotten by the lighthouse keeper who heard it, swearing night didn't matter where daybreak was proven. A misaligned echo: accounted for, in the gathering unlit of April, not yet forgiven.

Consigning ourselves to the ground that language incurred, we tacked our tents to what lack alone could affix: cutwater and floodwrack, breakwater and flame trees crazing dispersal, fir trees after a fire, the fire itself. Every word askew without rosetta or Ariadne's thread: *parousia, paroxysm, purlieu.* A scarlet tanager posed as red underwing, blue-eye as bluegill, grayling as rainbow trout, impromptu austerities mimicking rough, fermented baroque. Across the boundaries courting our diffusion, one voice eloped with another: discordant twins skirting the flimsy half-acres separated by wire, indebted to an outlaw weather flexing rudderless. Fly-rods leaning against the porch screen of a nearby tackle shop cast a maze of cuneiform and flense, the sun not shining except at night, by proxy, from the other side.

13

Asleep on the shattered surface of a cinematic, lunar creek, one of us dreamt the silhouette of a dog, yet found upon waking it hadn't strayed. Such were the spells of a landscape that couldn't be trusted although we'd devised it ourselves, if only to attribute otherwise: a zone where no one believed any longer the hollows that brought them this far, where flowers were blooming again, without any scent.

14.

Nor were we immune to such evolve and overwhelm. A diminishing match the frontier of unbreaking, we vexed oscura to spark, hearing it inhabit a new constellation: neither the sisters who cluster for beauty nor Sirius in a bid for omnipotence, but waxflower and ironbark, plainchant of a diesel engine coruscating rock at the edge of across. Where—razorwire spiraled to prevent the dead from defecting, or ghosts from insinuating when least required—a floodlamp brailled the salt flats torn from a page too charred to read, as we wagered who the photographer was, cutting our hearts on the hours until sunrise, on anything not expired. The soul opting out through its second-hand lens: the eye that eroded from lexis to shadow, azured by estrange, or the eye beset by a looking-glass inlet, a mile ago dark but now dazzling.

The only thing not lit the light itself. To draw the river in outline, orthography leafing a bayou trimmed by imaginative amours—even if mistaken for the real desire it honored by keeping close—the sun doubled back to offer its floreat, deception heating stanzas to crystal and shard. Nothing would crack this illumined facade, where we rowed one direction while facing the other, unmended and afraid. Later, the vanity of daytime brushing up as fireflies and crickets ignited, two stars that appeared to be moving turned out to be a plane, and the pilot, if there was one, couldn't see us: tangential to the current, we rested in its parallel until both wingflares joined, mystique dislimned by the intimacies of reserve. The heart, though hidden, had not stopped. We saw it out of the corner of eyes that did not belong to us: a tree that was once a woman, running into the sleight affray of one god denying another.

The preludes to morning were only a decoy: lemon trees rinsed in sidereal drowse, black swans and jasper reprising each other, the map a space for inventoried charades. Rorsch-ached to a po-faced noon, we tinkered with an engine that wouldn't catch, while the selves the sun repeated for us, aslant and appareled in zinc, unrehearsed their agitated angles of repose.

By night the barren floodways looked full, sand and surface tension the same. Dragonflies in the scarlet gorge were camouflaged as the gorge, while revenants appeared as their former selves, dressed in scarlet for carnival, to make love again under the ruined viaducts. The swimming hole ambered by alkaline dusk, heavy with muscat, unwavering depth, we barely stayed afloat, trimming an arc that blurred toward the cliff face, gathering into its blunt, cosmetic pall: umbrella bush and the harlequin clouds, gods who deferred out of weakness or contempt. Seismic lines were a narrow vein that syntax had carved and kept clear, fossil fuel deposits a pretext for conserving the unannounced. At sunset we sat on the rim of a crater half a mile across, where a baby had tipped from her cradle and fallen hundreds of years to the earth.

Clairvoyance of a harlot sky, milieu that staked its patient claim in white, amethyst, indigo, white. By the time the unsealed road was completed, its starting point was already in need of repair: weapons transport and railway sleeper replaced by quarry trucks, the wiper blades cut a suffix to the canyon, our lives a traffic concerning someone else, yet they were ours. The saw pit creek was pure itinerary, ironstone lagoon the color of port, of errancy. The mechanic who quit five months ago told us the weighbridge had snapped in a torrent, though we never spoke to him or saw the breakage in a whispered cicatrice. Stepping back, stepping farther back: perfumed shins of venus glade around us held us safe, all right with postponement, whatever its worth, hiking through the vulcan net, bathing one another in the falls.

Shrugging aside to reconvene in the rearview mirror, we drafted the vanishing point of a restive intent: a mission settlement vacant at the border, its burnt lime walls and flagstone floors the remnants of an interrupted gaze. But not these elements alone: the shearing shed wall and what echoes it would have assisted, a rainwater tank with a lilt but little rain, the chapel with crossbarred windows, an isolation ward. In the town outside the gate, seen from the slope of a trail to the power station, corrugated metal sheeting sent the sun back to its center, eschars in a rigged exchange of debt. We laughed in sync with a child playing hopscotch, whose mother, though counting for him, was far away. The onset of evening plied a mandarin motif: a hill in frenetic mascara, and a bat that circled galvanized iron roofs to unbalance the fronds, adding its weight to all that was not day.

Periphrasis, calligraphy. A motorcyclist moving in front of sound. The risk in her disappearance into earliest resolute dark. Our being seen by what we could not see, our guile and guilt. Solo that threatened to dissipate both piano and its player.

That we would provoke a nearness, sitting inside the sunlight knowing grass was no less sunlight, nor were we: there we found already we were wrong. What vicinity unconcealed itself between us—its disposition of cautious advance, rapids an assurance under the bridge—solicited the distance we sought to erase. Shoots enfolded in green, translucent foil, the ground evolved inarticulate parry and play, as rosebushes stood on their roses, roots awave in a zephyr, distracted by a formal mouth that moved, was moved upon. In disparity, a givenness conferred: cantus hailing a corner of winter, a summons pressed together and injured apart. To set a preposition at a vertical affording a view, to dance with parentheses, dance with a stone, to blind and be blinded by, to make up words for what would not otherwise enter and *fly in the face of*: we drew closer by drawing one pace away, turning forward, turning back again. Sun was only a legible smear of the absence it disguised: a shirt, a dress, the red of a cloud, this wounded thing that carried itself through the maiden, the missing snow. There was no hypocrisy in the forfeit thought of a door. That we would be as anabranch to each other: air that opens and closes in air, wind that opens and closes inside the wind.

What stick appear broken in water, what broken wood be whole.

The first planes left ahead of the sun, then light brought with it a language that could not speak of light. Inured to scant declensions of the solar, the lake was a manicured salina, insects glazed in hygienic veneer, as we waded out into childhood and chapter, up to our knees in a mirror crusting white. One plane had written a slogan across the sky, but wind had disfigured it, minutes before, to a name with the vowels excised. Driving back to the campsite after filming what wouldn't cohere, feral cats flayed and strung from a tree, wheels churned marbled dirt and gouache of the catchment's infirm edge, its perimeter a dog-fence inscribed like a score. Night failed to divert itself, and troubled the land and its listeners with keelhauled, anonymous noir: lineaments of a vandal alphabet, or the severed arm that drifted through our constant, captive sleep. In the static cool of three a.m., somebody coughed, awoke in a hurry, set about hoisting a pair of kerosene lamps—one to see the other by.

24

Strife of gravel and undertow, current against itself. Because
we hadn't looked behind, we could not find our way back:
invisible from the highway, its vaulted windows splintering
the maverick corals of light, a conservatory came into view,
upright and deflective as a phrase our conversation excluded,
that kept recurring in skewed coincidence. Inside, seated at a
table by herself, an infanta wearing a silk and ivory dress and
waving a fan, taking tea as if she were still alive: unfaithful
to August, the sun's arc, the seasons, inhabiting nowhere and
never and falling in love.

Its shadow also fell: shuttered within the sun's eye, a fallen, cimmerian oak. As the beekeeper woke to scrape out the combs, the pianist who'd lost an arm performed with the other: brittle spine of an irrigation hex, a citation the telegraph louvered and bleached, or the immolation and costumed veer of a tipsy, saracen light. Staggered across the desert, repeater stations forwarded lacunae and ciphers' skirl, a contour built by interval, by sounds distressed when written. A daughter digressed the crotch of a tree, and along the nowash zone: opal surf unhazarding, a harridan beach to lick its salt with salt.

Under arcades of snowgum and snow, a cerberus invigilating antiseptic thaw: glaciers that changed to ladders, anvils into ash. We could not tell what exactly it was, but we could see it was there, stenciling reluctant fog, razing the vestiges of an indigent dark: footsteps engraved in covert decorum, forest sienna and ochre with sleet, raffia grasses stopping at the cusp of shale, the shifting grade. Then moving across the pasture, pewter slush and emerald striae, as if to embrace our beveled remove from ourselves: it came of its own accord, pale like a naked body among the gravities of dawn, cleaning himself in the river, its blueness, the rumor of light after light. He stayed there through the afternoon, casting no shadow, neglecting to speak, never once turning to look at who loved him; and then, at dusk, he walked from the water into a soutache of stone. As the runaway sun divulged a mountain, by slipping behind its illusions of measure and immobility, we shouldered our semblance, place without place, awaiting another for whom we do not wait:

In "Viatica" 11, the phrase "a red flower, a good thrashing, a white and wooden overcoat" is from Baptiste in Marcel Carné's "*Les Enfants du Paradis.*" The sequence's closing question was asked by Brynne Rebele-Henry, age 2.

The epigraph to "Albedo" is from "The broken heart," from which two lines in 13 are likewise taken. The sixth line of 3 follows this description of the soul in Philippe Jaccottet's "*On Voit,*" from *Pensées sous les nuages* (Éditions Gallimard, 1983): "*punie de sa froideur par ce froid.*"

"Masquerade" is for Kevin Hart and Chris Wallace-Crabbe. The floating names in 6 are from Heraclitus. 13 is after Andrei Tarkovsky's "Stalker." The end of 17 recalls an Aboriginal tale. 18 is for Michelle Forrest and Kelly Cobb. 21 is for Judith Bishop. 22 is for Karin Christiansen. The end of 24 reprises one of Diotima's admissions in Friedrich Hölderlin's *Hyperion.* 26 is *in memoriam* Reverend Monsignor Charles A. Kelly (1942–2001).

Andrew Zawacki is the author of a book of poetry, *By Reason of Breakings* (2002), and a chapbook, *Masquerade* (2001), which received the Alice Fay Di Castagnola Award from the Poetry Society of America. He is coeditor of *Verse* and, as a fellow of the Slovenian Writers' Association, edited *Afterwards: Slovenian Writing 1945–1995* (1999). He earned a B.A. from the College of William and Mary, an M.Phil. from Oxford University, and an M.Litt. from the University of St. Andrews. He studies in the Committee on Social Thought at the University of Chicago.